What's it like to be a...
VETERINARIAN

Written by Judith Stamper
Illustrated by Marcy Dunn Ramsey

Troll Associates

Special Consultant: Bruce R. Wittels, D.V.M., *Mid-Monroe Veterinary Hospital, Monroe, New York.*

Library of Congress Cataloging-in-Publication Data

———
  What's it like to be a veterinarian / by Judith Stamper;
illustrated by Marcy Dunn Ramsey.
      p.   cm.—(Young careers)
   Summary: Describes the work done by a veterinarian as she treats a
variety of small and large animals.
   ISBN 0-8167-1817-2 (lib. bdg.)   ISBN 0-8167-1818-0 (pbk.)
   1. Veterinarians—Juvenile literature.   2. Veterinary medicine—
Vocational guidance—Juvenile literature.   [1. Veterinarians.
2. Occupations.]   I. Ramsey, Marcy Dunn, ill.   II. Title.
III. Series.
SF756.S73   1990
636.089′69—dc20   89-34391

What's it like to be a...
VETERINARIAN

"My puppy is sick," a boy tells the animal doctor.

Dr. Scott carefully takes the small dog into her arms. She is a veterinarian. It is her job to make sick animals well again.

"What is the puppy's name?" Dr. Scott asks.
"Bingo," the boy answers. "And I'm Ben."

"Come with me, Ben and Bingo," the
veterinarian says. "I'll see what the trouble is."

They walk into Dr. Scott's examining room.
The doctor puts the dog on a metal examining
table. Ben pets Bingo. The little dog looks afraid.

"This won't hurt, Bingo," says Dr. Scott. She
gently feels the puppy's stomach.

Then, Dr. Scott takes out the things she needs to examine an animal. She uses a thermometer to take the dog's temperature. She puts on her stethoscope next. It helps her listen to the dog's heart and lungs. Finally, she shines a small flashlight into Bingo's eyes and mouth. The puppy's throat is very red.

Suddenly, Bingo sneezes a puppy sneeze.
"Ah...ah...choof!"

Dr. Scott shakes her head and smiles.
"Bingo," she says, "you have a very sore throat
and a bad cold."
"Ah...ah...choof!" Bingo sneezes.

Dr. Scott goes to her medicine cabinet. She takes out some pills to help the dog's throat get better.

"Give these to Bingo three times a day," she tells Ben. "Try hiding the pills in some food," she adds with a smile. "Most puppies don't like medicine."

"Thank you," Ben says. He gathers Bingo
into his arms. "Dr. Scott," he asks, "how do you
become a veterinarian?"

"You must like animals and want to help them," the doctor explains. "And it takes at least eight years of college. That's a lot of studying and hard work—but it's worth it!"

After Bingo leaves, Dr. Scott is ready for her next patient. It is a gray-colored Siamese cat. The animal has come for its checkup. First, Dr. Scott weighs the cat. She keeps a record, or history, of the health of each of her patients.

Next, the cat is given its yearly vaccinations.
These shots keep animals from getting sick.
Finally, the doctor gives the cat's owner some
vitamins. Animals need vitamins to stay strong
and healthy.

Now it is time for Dr. Scott to visit the animals in her hospital. It is where sick animals stay. Every day, she checks her patients there.

A spaniel with a broken leg is in one of the
cages. It looks at Dr. Scott with sad, brown eyes.
"Cheer up, Bonnie," the veterinarian says.
"You'll be running around again soon."

Dr. Scott pulls two x-ray pictures from a file. The x rays show the bones inside the dog's body.

The x ray on the left was taken when Bonnie came to the clinic. It shows where the leg was broken. The x ray on the right was taken after Dr. Scott set the leg. It shows the bone healing.

Next, Dr. Scott checks on a mother cat. The doctor helped the cat have four kittens last night. The kittens are curled up close to their mother.

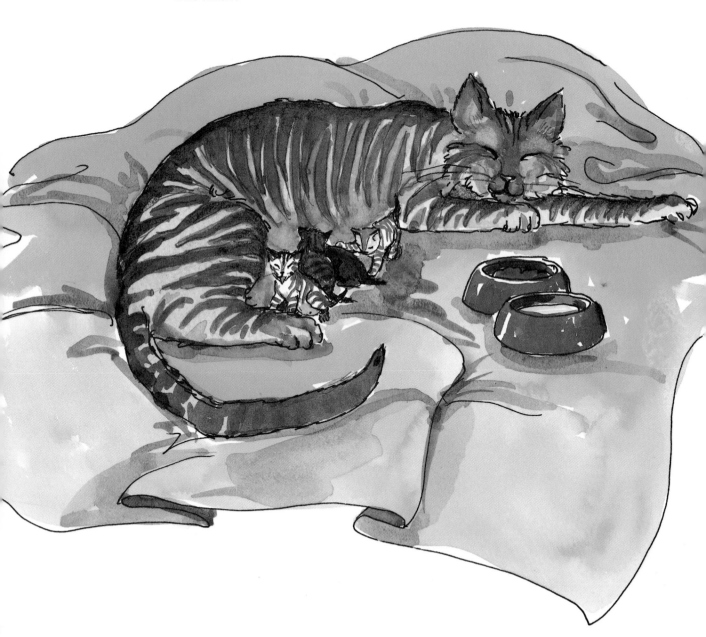

The veterinarian walks up to a big cage.
Inside is a white sheepdog named Snowball. The
dog had an operation yesterday. Dr. Scott checks
the stitches on the dog's stomach and takes its
temperature.

Dr. Scott takes a blood sample from the dog. She puts a drop of blood on a small glass slide. Then she studies it under a microscope. Everything looks okay. Snowball will be well again soon.

The veterinarian's assistant walks into the room. Dr. Scott tells her what food to give the sick animals. The assistant also gives the animals their medicine and keeps their cages clean.

Just then, the telephone rings. Dr. Scott goes to answer it. "I'll be over right away," she says. The owner of a horse farm has just called. A foal, or baby horse, is very ill.

Dr. Scott packs her medical bag. She puts in
her stethoscope, thermometer, and flashlight.
She also takes along a needle used for giving
shots, some pills, and medicine.

The veterinarian drives out of town to Green Hills Farm. Small pets can be brought to her hospital. But a veterinarian must travel to see large farm animals.

"Thanks for coming," the owner of the farm says when the doctor arrives. "The foal is in here." Dr. Scott follows him into a stable.

10999

The foal is lying on the straw. Its brown eyes are watering. Its breath is coming in short gasps.

Dr. Scott kneels down beside the foal. She takes the foal's temperature. Next she listens to its heart and lungs. Then she looks at its eyes and mouth.

"You called just in time," she says to the owner. "The foal has a bad lung infection. It needs a shot of antibiotics."

Dr. Scott takes out her needle and some medicine. She gives the foal a shot to fight the germs in its body. The young horse whinnies in surprise.

"I'll check back tomorrow," Dr. Scott says.
She gently strokes the foal's neck to calm the
animal.

Dr. Scott leaves the horse farm. She stops by her house for lunch. As she opens the door, she gets a welcome home.

"Me-e-e-ow!" her two cats mew.

"Ruff-ruff!" her Irish setter barks.

"Polly wants a cracker!" her parrot begs.

Dr. Scott laughs as her pets crowd around her. She has always loved animals. That is why she became a veterinarian.